NITRO NIGHTS

ALSO BY W.S. DI PIERO

POETRY

The First Hour

The Only Dangerous Thing

Early Light

The Dog Star

The Restorers

Shadows Burning

Skirts and Slacks

Brother Fire

Chinese Apples: New and Selected Poems

ESSAYS

Memory and Enthusiasm: Essays 1975–1985

Out of Eden: Essays on Modern Art

Shooting the Works: On Poetry and Pictures

City Dog

When Can I See You Again? New Art Writings

TRANSLATIONS

Pensieri, by Giacomo Leopardi

This Strange Joy: Selected Poems of Sandro Penna

Photography: A History

Ion, Euripides

Night of Shooting Stars: The Selected Poems of Leonardo Sinisgalli

W.S. DI PIERO NITRO NIGHTS

COPPER CANYON PRESS

PORT TOWNSEND, WASHINGTON

Cover art: Andrew Moore, *Red Chairs, Selwyn Theater, Times Square, New York, 1996* [1996]

Copper Canyon Press is in residence at Fort Worden State Park in Port Townsend, Washington, under the auspices of Centrum. Centrum is a gathering place for artists and creative thinkers from around the world, students of all ages and backgrounds, and audiences seeking extraordinary cultural enrichment.

LIBRARY OF CONGRESS CATALOGING-IN-PUBLICATION DATA

Di Piero, W. S.
  Nitro nights / W. S. Di Piero
    p. cm.
ISBN 978-1-55659-380-2
I. Title.
PS3554.I65N58 2011
811'.54—DC22

                    2011023817
98765432 first printing

COPPER CANYON PRESS
Post Office Box 271
Port Townsend, Washington 98368

www.coppercanyonpress.org

0 3148 6143

ACKNOWLEDGMENTS

Thanks to Wendy Lesser of *The Threepenny Review* and Christian Wiman of *Poetry*, who have long kept the screen door lit for me. "Movie Night" first appeared, in a different version, in *The Only Dangerous Thing* (1982, Elpenor Books). Some poems have been in magazines, most in different versions: "Only in Things," "The Shoe Box," "The Torch Singer," "That Night at Baldini's" in the *Harvard Divinity Bulletin;* "The Lives of Objects" in *MARGIE;* "A Lowrider Loudly Brings Us," "Sea to Shining Sea" I & II, "Sales," "The Girls, "Johnny One Note," "Big City Speech," "New Endymion," "Autumn and I Can't Breathe," "More Dreams and So What?" "Renovations" in *Poetry;* "Another Fourth" in *Poetry Northwest;* "Going in Circles," "Two Uncles" in *A Public Space;* "What Have You Got to Lose?" "Salt" in *The Rumpus;* "Their Old Knives" in *Slate;* "The Light Box" in *Subtropics;* "The Discovery of Glass," "The Invention of Photography," "Invocations to Fear" in *The Threepenny Review.*

No one
can understand what makes the present age
what it is. They are mystified by certain
insistences.

"Impromptu: The Suckers"
WILLIAM CARLOS WILLIAMS

CONTENTS

●

NITRO NIGHTS

•

Only in Things

Some days, who can stare at swathes of sky,
leafage and bad-complected whale-gray streets,
tailpipes and smokestacks orating sepia exhaust,
or the smaller enthusiasms of pistil and mailbox key,
and not weep for the world's darks on lights, lights on darks,
how its halftones stay unchanged in their changings,
or how turning wheels and wind-trash and revolving doors
weave us into wakefulness or dump us into distraction?
This constant stream of qualia we feel in our stomachs.
The big-leafed plant lifts its wings to greet the planet's chemistry,
the sun arrives on rooftops like a gentle stranger, rain rushes us
love to love, stop to stop, these veins of leaf, hand, storm and stream,
as if in pursuit of us and what we are becoming.

Another Fourth

Everything's shut, fireworks'
damp slamming somewhere
while I walk for hilltop vantage
to watch their milky flares,
so up 17th to nothing then
down to Market Street's trolleys,
looking for the heat. Deep fog pumped
by faraway ballpark light:
the closer I come,
the darker it gets, closer now
to midnight, public transit life
kicking up its soiled skirts.
Transvestite colts, Mexican
yard guys, an almost fight
between driver and citizen,
who you calling nigger, nigger,
off at Van Ness, wasted...
what anyway was I looking for?
How you feel? I ask
the elderly Indian gentleman
who stares at chewing gum
buttoned to his fingers.
I feel as fine as fog.
Tonight I'm sure to meet
a woman who wears red shoes.
I love this land.

A Lowrider Loudly Brings Us

a thing called radar love,
the whole hog calling us,
and here's unhoused Ginger,
distracted wind-beaten beauty
separating from park bench
and Frigidaire carton,
flying Halloween colors,
tie-dyes, orangesicle socks,
where will she sleep tonight,
where lay those tulle angel wings
slashed through her overcoat,
who pulses anarchist patchouli
and minty hair draughts
and cigarette spirits that scuff
our fragile air while we hope for
some pick-me-up before we pass.

Sea to Shining Sea (I)

Jamaican maintenance man, Trinidadian chambermaid, Haitian desk
clerk, the boss housekeeper African American, the counter-cadenced
musicality of their voices like dust devils in my Chicago hotel's air while
Presidential Campaign commentary snickers inside televisions inside
rooms. I linger in the lobby and hallways, tuned into the sweet sliding
parabolic vocalizing. Inside my room, cable's talking heads bark and
snarl in see-here tones, nowhere accents, Pentecostal and justified, but
they mean well. "The American people want what they want and they'll
get it." Outside the door, someone runs a vacuum. The falling leaves
drift past the window, autumn leaves of red and gold.

Sales

Miguel might, if he speaks English, call the colors
of ukuleles stretching their necks from yards
of canvas duffel yoked across his shoulders,
auroral azul, cherry pop, or mojito green,
under this Pac Heights sky where the awful rich
snap their heels past shop windows, past goatskin bags,
fibristic sheets of celadon paper from Zhejiang,
FIAT cremini, and Cinco de Mayo gelato.
Smiling past them, he passes with his happy load,
a display model whole and nude in his hand,
on sale to no one, uplifted like a Stratocaster
sacramental from mahogany forests in Paraguay.

The Day After Tomorrow

A woman in silk dressing gown carries fire in a brown paper bag.

Ravens silent on roof flashing and ridges lift one leg then another.

A car built of coal gleams in the sun near the bus stop and ignites.

Slimed water climbs sides of houses where the hundred ravens sit.

The sunset pools on housetops and liquefies the fog's groggy eye.

Magic time for the fire-bearing priestess and astute nervous ravens.

In one another's eyes we see endtimes in flames along the horizon.

On cornea and iris and roofs and trees the fatigued sun settles fast

into our blood that feels like heavy fire before the changes come.

Sea to Shining Sea (II)

A half-mile from the pueblo you see black smoke running up the nighttime sky, bright flecks chipping the firmament, stars so blissful oblivious and conscienceless they overcome us like the gods Greeks and other tribes believed them to be. Inside the pueblo, piñon bonfires blaze, sparks fly into children's hair and parkas, flames shave off from the core of the fires and rise to the stars like propitiation. Bonfires burn in such darkness that you expect sacrifice to happen, while inside the adobe chapel an evening children's service hums, then the procession exits bearing statues of Christ and Mary around a long slow circuit of the pueblo. It's not just the darkness and the firestorm-fear of hot winds in cold December air, not just this, but the elemental bodily presence of belief, submission to what's irretrievably yonder and what's only here, that makes you feel you could lose yourself, you could go up in smoke and only later will friends realize you're missing.

The Girls

Eighteen sixty-one eighteen sixty-five,
six hundred ten thousand men
gaseous gray, blackened body parts
like chopped wood in Virginia sunshine.
Or nineteen-fourteen nineteen-eighteen,
trench rats, thousands, big as badgers,
rip chines from horse and human flesh.
Cluster bombs, punji sticks, IEDs,
primed to shred feet, thighs, spine, sack
yesterday, when we were countless.
Conscience says Count them up and be good,
suck on me like red candy stick
in dropped lookaway moments.
Protected by neighbors, two girls
villagers know to be deficient
doll themselves up as bombs
for market day's lentils and yams,
and their protectors fly into parts
like a world-body neural surge.

Going in Circles

Here's a George Raft rat speeding above the subway's sacred hot rail
it returns to night after night for its fair share of peels, corn chips, and
smoothie blemishes, and I feel inside the all-at-once we can imagine but
not really know, as if in this moment a Cincinnati congregation awaits a
wordless voice to speak to them from ciborium or tabernacle while an
Old Oraibi ancient carves his bole of cottonwood into the kachina who
brings August's harvest gifts of gourds and corn to children gathered
in the plaza at daybreak, when painted gods dance to the world's four
corners while choirboys in Harlem sing that they may walk in the sway
of the Lord, the subway screaming here under their feet.

The Scarf

You lose your way—on a sidewalk, in a dark wood, jamming with whatever comes your way—you're dizzed, you jaywalk, the convertible hits the brakes and rocks, you get probation again, lucky you. Being lost is free fall, you're out of control, any morning you wake to a day or condition of soul, sensation so heightened that it awes and frightens. Foliage whisking outside the window sounds like breakers hissing and beating the beach. Birdsong so tinnily amped it seems aberrant, a player piano's *Moonlight* Sonata, more inside the skull than out. Bus doors hiss shut like pressure valves exploding. An airplane and its neutrinos so high and silent they look about to evaporate. Everything scarily keyed up and you feel exposed, flensed, but swaddled, too. Your ears mute the sound and resonance of your own voice. Speak and you're talking into a scarf.

Johnny One Note

(Bobby Hutcherson in Oakland)

The mallet strikes but something's off,
and so he hits again, curling that lower lip,
purses his brow, as if this sign, this minor woe,
were speech the vibes might understand,
so when he lifts bluish lids as if wakened
to the desired tone that rings now, it seems,
it sounds, under wraps, a water-ly quaver,
through the club crowd's silence,
as it floats above us like an aerosol
trying to find a new way to escape,
passes through the wall's mortared pores
to reverb in the cool night air of an un-
peopled sidewalk, droning toward the tracks
where a passing peopled train sucks up
and winds his finally found, wowed tone
around its wheels, held there by steel heat
one hundred miles, until it reaches the sea,
where wheels and whistle overreach
surging surf the good vibration feels
such desire for, and leaves its tedium
of the round and round, lofting to a sea
that comes and goes but finally simply goes,
as one night, this night, the cool vibes' air
(struck finally in the changed groove of sax
and ecstatic kit) is free, finally free,
to go where we won't hear from it again.

The Discovery of Glass

Before Venice's blowpipes and their estuarial ephemera, their hippogriffs
and crocs and chimeras, before Legos, aluminum foil, Blondie's heart,
and baggies, we'd seen dolphins in the spindrift, all smiles and blessings
loping alongside our trading routes as we hove to some tidal river shore
in Syria before sailing home to Phoenicia's girls and oils. The dolphins'
arc cut a wake, a disembodied perfection their magical bodies brushed
upon the air, a memory sea spray erased. That was before we camped
and a slave brought soda bricks from the cargo to build a stove for our
pots and crummy food. Have you seen the fish of the deep as some
travelers testify? Not undine or pistrix, but of the deepest deep, in the
dark down there, transparent blades and spheres, like glass, because
that's what they are, what we found there on the beach, fire cooking soda
and sand till both swam away like a greenish asp. The jeweled fluid ran
like flame itself liquefied and with no help from us assumed the shape of
the dolphins we'd seen, their lunette leap spread flat on the beach, which
form, land-bound, stopped and stayed with us.

The Master's Workshop, circa 1560

Today our minor master needs
angels for an *Assumption*
so hangs from wires wax slugs
modeled into spidered seraphs,
then roughs out shouting,
wing-heavy enthusiasts
scaled to a desired beefiness.
The more these higher orders
look like us, the nearer we are
to them—he really believes
this ripe glitter-glass illusion
of fleshly ghosts plunging
arrogant into our animal air,
even when a dunce apprentice
moves the candles and chunks
that seem to rise and fall at once
begin to melt onto his worktable,
liquefied wings and torsos falling
as angels are meant to fall
into the sacred scene, dripping,
inert now, recast into craters,
puddings, islands, fresh models
of what we've always been.

"Recurrent Obsession to Make Objects Move"

from Joseph Cornell's diaries

They lean into the husky Motorola,
into Satie's tunnels, Debussy's blue lights,
Astoria's air pastes summer on windowpanes:
Joseph and his homebound brother, all smiles,
while chateau vines crawl up the basement walls,
rings zizz on rods, soap bubbles poof from pipes,
the Medici Prince and starlet woo in the dark.
A nice cheese Danish or cream éclair for lunch
washed down with powdered lemonade. Why leave?
Not him, not the palsied brother he loves too much
to leave, and besides, the sopranos and Ping-Pong balls
sigh in the basement while music's silks
and cautions slinky down, uncanny owls
stare out behind pink sequined winter trees...
Penny slots, cockatoos, zowie, and bare bulb
to light the blue wallpaper horoscopes.

The Invention of Photography

The adenoidal, glass-brick fifties,
Tarʒan featured on the cell block
for Moyamensing's livid inmates,
doing their screening room shuffle,
while Uncle P. talked to a guard
and I feared things that they did not.

●

In the fearless 1850s, mad-hatters forged
images of dolls, doilies, sewers,
eight-year-old odalisques
in off-the-shoulder nighties…
Gentleman Brits claimed their Sphinx
and Hindoo temples. We had our Civil War,
rail cuts and silver mines,
darkroom vans racked with plates,
jerky, mule feed, cameras
the Sioux called shadow catchers.

●

Pull the lens cover,
the ground glass blinks a century
to a two-minute wonderment,
when every decent family craved
its Polaroid and waited to see what
it would make of us, how inhale
blood matter, lick it into life.

●

The string-bean screw says, "poor creeps,"
and leads us through stone
MGM Egyptian gates
to sunlight's harsh hurrah outside,
shows off his sedan's crimped,
toasted fender that Uncle P. shoots
for insurance evidence, then,
more evidence, a conversation piece:
me, guard, and penitentiary.

●

I later found inside a drawer
a foxed sixties print. A secret
about a secret. Sunday morning,
there they stand, fertile forms,
grinning, hamming it up,
uncle, wife, and son,
a standardized toxic family
the squeezebox resolved into color,
still a little liquid with the past:
they stare into the yonder yonder,
with no hint of the old eternity
we all heard so much about
in the church conspiring behind them,
or eternity's simulacrum
where convicts served their time.

●

Fast times now lead us through
our small malarial wars for the millions,
platoon grins, cemetery symmetries,
a bullet in a flattened head, dead men's dumps,
Pol Pot's carefully numbered portrait archive,
the fallen and the disappeared from city towers:
a double-page spread, a yearbook layout.

●

But now here we are in Sharon Meadow,
pixeled in the viewfinder screen
by an accommodating stranger,
we and background congas and bongos
shrink-wrapped in the sky's irradiated green.
We smile for the moment filed away.

●

Now, love, tip your laptop screen.
Now we see us, now we don't,
digital daguerreotype spooks,
chromed noses, iridium eyes,
who fade, just so, to slate or silver.
We lie in wait there for ourselves.

Two Uncles

Mister Mister

As if he once was someone's son
but not now. He's the carpet slippers
guests hear scratching overhead
to big-band screech trumpet
rinsing from the ceiling.
Nobody asks. A chair leg
beats time on the floor,
how good he was, so quiet
those years and, why,
he's still here, upstairs,
who seemed so far,
how could we forget
the teacup outside his door,
the broken bologna sandwich,
canned tomato soup, man-boy
who once upon a time sat
calmly under Nate the barber's
long womanish pinky nail,
scissors hinting at his ear,
now our melancholy fatso
archangel of whom we ask
is Uncle Joe or Chazz or Luca
the same hopeless case?
What have we done
to make us suffer thus for him?

Dear Saint Jude, send him aid
from that smart cathedral shrine
in your far home in Florida.

Migraine Mike

Holy ogre of the basement,
pillow under the leg
trimmed by a panzer shell,
pouched speechless
in a wet web of pins
about his eyes and head.
Wife, mother, daughters
in Looney Tunes
shag slippers shuffle
overhead, woeful,
not to upset
the sleepless creature
or opioids nodding off
in cedar closets where
his 1940s Chesterfield
hangs like a haunter above
buffed brown-on-whites,
breathing tropical climes.
They shot the stump with morphine.
The headache dope don't work.
What drug can ever
suck Satan's blood
from iron-fisted Mike,
who keeps his women in line

and feels no phantom pain
when needles strobe his eyes?

St. Agnes Hospital Archive

Ike

See these scars? Like razor cuts. Dead palms.
The navy wanted volunteers,
so I went to rescue guys in Alaska,
we went far out, brought them back, you bet,
ropes, pack ice, axes, what have you.
My hands got frostbit, sliced like bacon.
I don't have to feel to carry things but Doc
was giving up, on the toilet, and man
has a dignity, you'd think, and he squirmed
like a loose hose, an eel, so, sorry I yelled,
I didn't know it was your first day standing.
Sammy digs you, says you looked funny,
not ha-ha but like a picture that's crooked,
leaning on the wall the way you did.
"Help! Here!" I'm sorry, it cracked me up.
Doc was gone anyway. You wanted to run
and gather a posse for sure. Here! Here!
You'll get your legs back someday, maybe.
That's just me talking. I'd bet on it, though.

Samantha

I call you my boy toy,
my hot ruined Casper,
the girls at the station,
they fall down laughing.
Tell me if I rub too hard,
the alcohol can burn you up.
Doc Cohen's really nice,
but he's all bone and Jell-O
and doesn't deserve how bad
she treats him. Shy, like you,
and I'll bet he never lets on
how his wife wakes him up,
got a gun to his head,
or hers, poor thing. Us,
we'll get close when you're out.
You need a little loving...
So get those legs back,
I'll take you clubbing,
we'll hit the Boat, or Pep's.
That woman, I don't know
how some people don't like life,
plus they're moneybags.
She sticks her head in the oven,
turns on the gas and waits,
just like that, you know,
while he's lifting the garage door.

Sully

You need a haircut more than a bear needs sleep, young man.
You let it grow so long, you're a love kid—you'd last
two minutes max inside. Long-haired freaks, get outta my way,
but everybody's got a right. The difference between manslaughter
and murder, first or second degree, I'm here to tell you,
is intent, and you try proving that. I never thought
there was much difference. At least I learned a trade,
which is more than I can say about the creeps inside,
not like, though, I could walk into any shop, get a chair,
hold a razor, once I'm out of here, which makes it sound
like there's no difference, hospital or jail, go figure,
like some people say, college people some of them,
like you. They're right, except for one big difference:
that there's a *difference*. You want a shave, too?
Just kidding. Lookee here, hands like rocks.

Ike

My hands work okay, but don't you talk about
that fellow's head Sully broke a beer bottle on
and killed him dead. At a wedding is what I heard,
he had serious drink in him, that's the key to the city.
Why he talked so much to you, I don't know,
he don't talk much to me or nobody. Talked to you
because, bet on it, he knew you couldn't just get up
and walk away. You're a lucky cripple, bet that one.
He'd cut anybody's throat for a nickel and a smile.

Doc

Paris was beautiful and I was young,
a GI who'd never even left Philly,
but we who lived to see it were alive,
and like those girls in cotton shifts
the breeze pawed, *I* wanted to paw...
You didn't have to touch to know
how you'd always remember them.
But the camps, our first look inside,
made me a Jew all over again.
Your poetry, I used to read poetry,
has words for evil, but what can it do
except name it, then name it again?
Eye sockets, you remembered them most.
Eyes that shall never open with wonder again.
I actually thought those words
but knew what a punk thought it was.
Et in Arcadio ego, kiddo, right?
I despaired of us, killers yawning
at their tasks, grooving evenings
to Schubert or Mozart. And there I was,
the helpless healer, a big joke, belief
bled from my heart. Now look at me,
banal drama queen, the dying darling,
sick at heart, heartsick, heartsore. So what?
I'm nobody's fool, or God's fool maybe.
Those summery girls, the bunk-racks,
all those damned bones and so-called showers...
I shipped home. My bride was waiting
and cried in our dark kitchen for weeks.

Sea to Shining Sea (III)

Shaken awake, get my ticket punched, time feels columnar and the
vertigo makes me shiver: March, riding the New York–to–Boston
Regional, my San Francisco air back home pounded by rainstorms that
scroll hillsides more tightly green while things here get whippy and
skinny with the season's denials. The same liquid intimacy with trains
as when I rode a musty Pullman with an aunt taking me to a ball game.
No, the circus. Evergreens washing past the window, the only tickle of
color a witch hazel's yellow leaf-sprouts in a Boston backyard. New
York to there, outside my window: the ruined stripped rafters of silver
maple and oak mark time for the huffy wheels, the landscape stripped,
ghastly, then improbably lush with firs that look even more plaintive
for all that browned-out scarcity. A stream's late winter light flashes
like tinsel rashed by Christmas lights, inlets along Rhode Island's
coastline sluggish, silvered. The train's sliding pulse runs through what
passes yet separates thing from thing, frame by frame, without giving
up the imagery's streaky swipe through time. Then a mash of birches
with clenched tops. Pines reduced to the horizontals of their branches,
scorings, staves in the air, a swift lyric continuity, then an old fallen stone
wall, talus, and scree. In the club car, while I'm watching twiggy speed
scratch the windows, behind me the hostess shouts: "Paterson!"

Nitro Night

What? "*Nitro* night's what this is." Strangers all, in the Haight and Fillmore bus shelter that shelters nobody and a voice cantors: "Like nitro*glyc*erin. *Boom!* Or like *ni*trate night." Poppers, photographic plates, laughing gas, you know, headshrinking. Plain life is complex and it's shrunk to the corner tonight. My bus is coming, I'm counting on it and in the meantime inhale seedy bump-elbows smelliness and love, smell the love, these vintage clothing stores, beery dives, Memphis Minnie's BBQ, Fade Specialist barbershop. Tonight's air gaslamped, trashy like TV on-the-spot spots. One corner: an Indian restaurant I've never seen anyone enter or leave, before its portals Black Muslims in militant bow ties and dark narrow suits distributing pamphlets. Gutterpunks shake chains and leer at them. Their Rottweiler leers. The Fruit of Islam stare back. The dog stands still. A woman across the street (summery dress, hair loosely pinned up) denounces and denounces. Twenty people mousing around the corner but none exist for her. And why is fatso leaning so long on the municipal trash receptacle? Ah, his pud hosed over the trashcan's lip is pissing a strong stream. Did he vote in the last election? He, too, studies the bow ties. Walt Whitman's Mannahatta and Brooklyn and Camden, Civil War draft-riot lynchings, manure everywhere, sidewalk vendors, open streetside fires, chickens running loose in certain neighborhoods. A white limo pulls up, a youthful personage in running gear jumps out and runs into a café while a squad car stops behind the limo and its jellybean bar washes the windows: he squirts from the café, waves his arms in mock-appeal, the driver steps from the limo while the cruiser whines, "Stay in your vehicle," the speechifying lady cool toward the cops declaims some more, the Muslims at attention regard the whole hang-time scene, and my bus is nowhere in sight.

Big City Speech

Use me
Abuse me
       Turn wheels of fire
       on manhole hotheads

Sing me
Sour me
       Secrete dark matter's sheen
       on our smarting skin

Rise and shine
In puddle shallows
       under every Meryl Cheryl Caleb Syd
       somnambulists and sleepyheads

Wake us
Speak to us
       Bless what you've nurtured in your pits
       the rats voles roaches and all outlivers
       of your obscene ethic and politics

Crawl on us
Fall on us
       you elevations that break and vein
       down to sulfuric fiber-optic wrecks
       through drill-bit dirt to bedrock

Beat our brows
Flee our sorrows

    Sleep tight with your ultraviolets
    righteous mica and drainage seeps

        your gorgeous color-chart container ships
        and cab-top numbers squinting in the mist

What Have You Got to Lose?

Third-floor walk-up, simple morning
complex with possibility.
Where will I find my garden?
Where wild roses for the darker hours?
Or yellow roses for safekeeping
to light these shadowed rooms
until tomorrow, when on the streets
Scotch broom and mimosa bloom
in ambivalent greeting winds...

Having My Cards Read

Hoboes wail a garbage can against
the cyclone links. The monkey puzzle tree
droops its scaly tails above our heads
as she sets up near the zoo's bonobos,
humping happy in their cages close
to chimps ripping off each other's ears.
And in the cloud reposing on the sky,
cut by an F-22's long hookah puffs,
the cyan atmospherics rupture into
solarized platelets: her Ray-Bans foil
my own face back at me:

> *A time of renewals*
>
> *though somewhere*
>
> *dark cold woe*
>
> *You won't know what's what*

Comes a taste of sea to make her pause,
and marine gusts slice and spook her cards, my cards,
that flurry to the sidewalk, near the barred gate,
breaking fortune down faster as she speaks.

The Lives of Objects

1. On My Worktable

They are some other life,
the seagull skull, salt flight,
speed and glide
and baffled braincase
holding lost fire,
keeping its secrets
beyond the time
passing through me now.

The Zuni wolf fetish
out of its old sacred story
among Brother Badger,
Sister Skunk,
pointing its muzzle
at this Bronx Zoo photo:
a sexed-up couple
watched by the wolf
in its concrete pen
caged by ashy shade.
Come to us, we say
to things so close to us.
Be of us. Help us know
what you know.

Fulvio, hitching penniless
with bad men in Sudan,
found this terra-cotta shard,

kept it for twenty years,
coptica probabilmente…
Cavafy in his Alexandrian room
inhales heavy phantoms
of an afternoon's hurried sex,
orange rinds, and coffee dregs
his bourse-trader bedmate
sips somewhere now
with somebody else.

I dust and re-arrange them
in their fussy disorder.
Speak to me,
conch heart, inkpot,
brainy coral, bring me
the all-at-once.
Maculate flakes fall
on the Ferris wheel
when I topsy-turvy
the globe her hands held
(*woman much missed,*
how you call to me, call to me)
like an offering to now,
when she'd be gone.

And on still-wet tiles
Mayan slaves incised suns,
jaguars, faces, parasols,
bricked them into walls
unseen until the jungle
dragged the walls to ruins

I'll never see but for
the fragment beside this page,
this hand, another elsewhere
far from my heart beating
this early ochre morning
that bakes the bones
under my skin flayed
by the hour I live in.

2. *Not On My Table*

Pumped pinup tits
on yearbook stock
Father taped inside
his locker: coveralls,
painter's cap, Camels,
cherried medicine-bottled
flaky wine he drank
by the drive-in speaker
that rained-on night
at *Pork Chop Hill.*

Mother's chiffon blouses,
zircon pendant,
henna dye-packs,
organdy nail polish,
dream book, Mass cards,
freebie serving spoon
from the Point Breeze
movie house featuring

one rainy afternoon
The Robe and *Ivanhoe.*

The Light Box

Three a.m. moonshine boxed on my kitchen floor.
Spastic, sleepless, heavy, too full of metals
when what I need is air or fire,
I wait for daylight to start me up:
full moon, corpulent air, fog teased
through streetlights, then the news-photo world
of piping crimped like dead mosquitoes,
shredded drywall, kids with stumps, Humvee treads
like mashed lizards, white smoke boiling white dust.
My book says King Leopold's best earners,
to prove who refused to harvest Congo rubber,
brought baskets of black hands like dead toads.

Headachy with change he claims to love,
wishing lesser seriousness, oh if only,
there he crudely stands, this monkey *me*,
vigilant, inert, beyond belief.
The moon passes our passing planet.
At his railroad flat's far loveless end,
the scratched skylight's beam
crushes lunar fibrillations to a perfect,
pale circle too small to stand inside.
Thus he drags across the tubercular round
his shadow's puny laughable fatigue
and has his late night moment in the sun.

April

It isn't good to have too much.
Good lies, I tell myself, in having less.
The rain that cuts the sun's dense rays,
a look that feels too much like touch
in too many places, the heart's fine distress
that perfume brings, or sight, or taste.

I wake and have to check my haste
to suck her juices, his love, their faith,
taking what I know they won't offer,
the leafy trees and wisteria like wraiths…
Love and touch shouldn't take such effort
this season, when nothing goes to waste.

New Endymion

She visits still too much, dressed in aromas
of fir needles, mango, mold: I still get lost
knowing she's close, me not getting younger
or more conscious. Sometimes I fantasticate
I'm broad awake: her witchy presence waits
for me to jump into her arms, but then she's just
an incoherent ache in sleep's freaked scenes.
I feel her frosty nitrogenous hands and wrists
vaporing nooses around my head and feet
and genitals, conjuring my drab hair
into a party bowl of oiled, desirable locks.
She makes me nervous, but what would I do
without her? So long as I can't have her,
I want her and this alarming manic frequency.
Then again, who wants to wake to change,
its pulped, smelly suit of meat, drawing flies?
My night-watch hot girl, moon-maiden, mom,
let me get just one night's sleep without regret,
released from your foxy ticklish fondlings,
your latest smell of windblown fresh-cut grass.

Autumn and I Can't Breathe

1

Too much increase and pressured air,
sugar maples and oaks choked up
with cereal reds and oranges,
last apples to market, persimmons...
Two falls on two lakes. Flying over
Chicago's chunky silken skyline afloat
on Lake Michigan's slate prairie,
while over the Wannsee a harvest moon
lights my room, shrinks to a watery
seam as ducks and coots skid
like vaudevillians on deepening ice
to chase food no longer there.

2

Across Chicago's black horizon
Canada geese skid and bark,
grave clouds tamping their call.
There they go, Sarasota-bound,
homing closer in on the home
of John Ringling, O welcome me, too,
as you did those affluent Munchkins
who retired there. Thus the birds
come back in my thoughts like thoughts
though not as streaky, cranky, or fresh

as flocks we heard at Lake Champlain,
where we had that third autumn I forgot.

3

The softer, fooling fall we feel still lives,
because it's Indian summer, my friend,
and that overshadowed year, in canoes,
we chased their soundtrack nearly to
New York, the water stiffer as we rowed,
slowing us from finding a loud flock
we knew had to be closer when
they oared the air farther away,
and left us there, paddling fools,
sweating harder back to our safe shore,
to its thinner trees and falling leaves.

The Shoe Box

A high school mash note's stammering lust.
Father and me, shirts and ties, snapshot glare,
and somehow graphed into that air
a young man's foolscap poem when a just,
loose joinery of words was all that mattered.
But then in last night's dream, she (mother, wife,
mash note's love?) tells me a box holding secret life
has been shipped, enclosing sounds I haven't heard:
a wind-harp's warp, words yarding across staves,
fluty sounds ribboned to sad, screechy tunes.
And things: a wishbone, ring, whatever I crave,
the heart-hollows, the cannot-do-withouts, the whens
and whos, the frayed veils between death and here…
I packed this box myself. I packed it full of fear.

Invocations to Fear

Mon. You were awake all night while I wasn't. Now we can hit the streets together. Where and what would I be without you, joy's twisted twin? You both bring a rush. Stay with me as we go, stay a few steps behind.

Tues. I turn the corner and he sticks a gun in my belly. Well, there you are, as you were. The gun, the guy (Crazy Leo), the corner, the 8th grade dance I was leaving, the dark blown out of proportion by the moon, a streetlamp spotlighting Leo. What an aura. Occasion specific, you're easier to accommodate. You were just hawking that moment, like plenty of others. They come and go. But the barely audible ongoing drone of dread all day every day, the furtive fraughtness of it, makes the viscera curl, you devil you. Everybody has a personalized Leo. The dread's a specialization.

Wed. Saturating things as you do, whatever happens adds to your store of possibility. Whatever isn't there, whatever is, can become you, turn into you. I do love it when things don't go your way, when you go green-eyed because I'm mysteriously struck with Emily Dickinson's sourceless, untraceable joy that's "reportless, also, but sincere as Nature or Deity," even if the transport lasts only as long as it takes to say that. Then there you are again, watching my back.

Thurs. You smell bad. I don't much mind the flakey, wallpaper-paste nimbus you sometimes carry around, but today's rank gutter-oil stink means you're too close, too close for comfort. Did I say keep your distance? Shall I sing for you, sing you into submission, whistle you away, catcall your unknowingness, all the behind-the-doors and unnameable seizures of heart and body you afflict us with?

Fri. Listen up. I'll recite from my commonplace book. First Wm. James: "I went one evening into a dressing-room in the twilight to procure some article that was there; when suddenly there fell upon me without any warning, just as if it came out of the darkness, a horrible fear of my own existence." And his crony Royce, who loved looking at the night sky as a boy: "I came to seem so far from home; and the contemplation of the mere magnitude of Being gave me a choking in the throat, and a lonely kind of fear, – a fear which seemed all the more hopeless because nothing that I could conceivably do, or could pray God to do, or could hope for, could be expected to alter in the least the essential situation, or make this cold world of the beautiful stars and the terrible distances comfortably smaller." The words inoculate me? Fat chance. You live in the passions, not the head, uncontrollable you, even when I think I've wrestled you down, especially then.

Sat. Explosions, dust, families cowering outside houses that look like broken crockery, men in streets with casual rifles at their sides looking over their shoulders at the camera—your good-morning newspaper greeting. Smoke, charred plaster, rebar like exposed wiring in faraway places we'll never visit, but no matter, you make your point. Page 15, high schoolers gun down their chums, affectless cons sit on death row for decades, possibility of blizzard, mudslide, cataracts and hurricanoes, and fearless cretins with executive power killing suavely, on the q.t., very hush-hush. You're so bad, you spread this a.m. glaze across the soul, this slick we wear all day that dyes the day, and we're not even aware it's happening. What's your party affiliation?

Sun. Be what makes me what I am but be not the all of me. Shake my heart in just circumstances. Be lawless law and serve me. Of love be tender, love be sweet. Never let me go.

The Torch Singer

Career comeback, really wired, they said,
freshened, before you went out the window
like the hothead cop in that Italian film,
a goon-squad beat-down star
who one night, alone in his drab flat,
pours himself out his own window
on the world, like you, damaged
migratory angel, pure bent beauty
chained to a dead soul.
The dead tell what they know:
nothing at all—they can't
relieve our uncertainty.
How could you, they all said.
Planning another tour.
Maybe a CD. Who knew?
Puzzled weeklong laments and obits
by pals and literarios, ah,
canaries now with newfound tunes
deeper in the mine, who revise
the plot: true, though, for weeks
you hadn't left the apartment,
never picked up the phone,
but who expected *that?*
The gods don't get the blues:
their sulks and falling furies
don't consume their nature,
and melodrama irks them.
Life's got no shapeliness,

it crowds and pours from windows

like broken hourglass sand,

like your "It's All Over Now,"

sick sweet and there's nothing like it.

(Susannah McCorkle: 1946–2001)

Salt

The bread tastes funny, you said at dinner downstairs, before we climbed the floating stairs to the monkish loft, balancing ourselves shoulder to shoulder up to the narrow bed. Monopoly that deprives makes certain people rich. Florence's bakers quit salting bread when the Medici stiffened taxes. No salt since. The floured snow falling had held our tracks about as long as it took to open the apartment door. To go with the bread, I fixed savories—salami-ish, olivey, right?—with fried eggs and nasty lovable peperoncini. Dante says exile's bitterest taste is the salt in someone else's bread. One night was all we really wanted or needed. Just that taste. After we'd stepped to the loft, balancing palm on palm, you reminded me that he also said, let us not forget, along with that salt business, it's just as painful to have to go up and down someone else's stairs.

Talking Back

However awful or inauspicious the language I hear in sleep's rubied scenes, when those shape-shifting creatures call to me I know they want an answer, so even while waking I answer, I talk and talk and am actually speaking to my bedroom ceiling or into my pillowcase's deepening spelunk, and oh I do go on and feel the words bobbing along a current stroked by the dreaming life of me. *Here, take these cookies,* she-of-the-dream says. It's a counter girl, a revenant starlet type. Thanks, they're good. She's so grateful for my gratitude that she clasps my hand, and I cover hers with mine but hers isn't really there. It's flesh, it's not flesh, and I dread we're all dummies speaking an unconscious that owns us. I once woke vocalizing Italian, like practicing scales, and tried to spell out the ingredients and prep for the *spaghetti all'aglio e olio* we shared one midnight. Some morns I wake beseeching—don't take your hand away, don't scorch the pepper flakes, bring back that high—and keep going in the hope it will call back the vision, you and the food, the conversation's nacreous stage set. *Did you just say nacreous? You never say nacreous.* Well, this is the new me, I'm a changed man opening a changed mouth that leaks drool, like speech's condensation, a watermark to go with the areolate remnants of semen, menstrual blood, and olive oil droplets from those nights that were real and now unreal revisiting me, but by now I'm far out of the dream and shutting up, getting up, unlike the morning I lay awake for a while crooning the Five Satins' "In the Still of the Night" to that other side, longing to have it back, the one I'd left, singing see-you-later.

Movie Night

The Christmas Eve we missed our border train connection—
its details, like branches on a window, still tick in the mind:
stuck in that Alpine station till six a.m., your giggle fit
trying to pronounce Domodossola (*"Parigi'*s easier"),
clouds slurred over shingled railbeds, the yellowish café
a place for locals and transients to get a drink and news.
The zinc bar ignored the light, smoke warped a mirror
that looked scuffed by years of restoring the present.
Empty distracted bentwoods twisted away from tables,
and we imagined sleepless strangers, like us, who sat.
I stood in ashen shade, ordered coffee, and felt breath
lisp and honk behind my ear, the tall, heavy-lipped boy,
sooty circles under eyes looking hard at me. Right?
His lips hung open, chin glassy with spit, this is how
I remember it, how I want to restore to you this opaque gift
that slides across the moment while you're on your way
to pick me up for a movie in town… He grabbed my cup
and knocked the coffee down in one loud gulp,
staring at me as someone he never knew yet remembered
some vague harm I'd done him, who knows where?
Evil-eyeing me, as you tugged my coat the way you do
whenever I slide into the car beside you, as if to pull me
from harm's way, but now our train has finally arrived.

More Dreams and So What?

If only they didn't bleed
this mess into today's
first open-shuttered images,
and you weren't stepping
from some sawdust gantry,
or jungle tree-house, or
platform with "Lady Godiva"
on her high horse
above the Steel Pier tank
Atlantic City, 1955,
twenty years before
I tasted your breath
scented with paprika
and cumin, but in dreams
nothing's negotiable—and then
as I wake, you seem
to step down from the heights
fresher and more tactile than life
to lay your nakedness
the length of mine—
your speech sounds like
dry cracked feet rubbing
whitely at toe and heel,
an utterance of dark sand
of Ravenna's coast, ca. 1973,
or damp, kelp-whipped
Pacific sandstone beach
chunked between your toes…

More scenery: ice plant,
tide-pools, starfish
(so adherent and faithful!),
periwinkles, anemones
that like us shiver shut
at the faintest touch:
I wish the scenic didn't
seem to be all that is,
but the sea lion pup
stranded on a low-tide rock
telescopes its neck and head:
"Anybody there? I'll sing
a song for supper."
Its coat slips and slides
unattached to bone and muscle,
as experience slides
loosely around our flesh,
the wind's grains combing
its back and ours, as we,
in this high-strung dream
I'm waking from,
come at the same time,
crying out to sea,
but the vision is already
passed. Don't go, I say to
the dream's toil, to you,
don't go (another cry!)
you who didn't stay.

Narcissus in New Mexico

The gray-haired golden boy, still here, still doesn't know
he's dead to the world, his sparser curls crisped with snow.
The voice he thinks he hears once wove itself like chords
strummed through piñon pine and aspen, birds that slap
through leaves and trees, and wind that washes her old words
against his useless ears. In the riverbank's remnant ice-glaze,
soiled with ferns and grit, he sees the fatigued, opaque face,
so vigilant all winter, waiting for a finer, clearer beauty there,
amazed to outlast freshness he thought would never end.

The frosted sheet holds tawny clouds dragged by wind,
violet sunsets, shades of large birds contracting around
his heavier head. Underneath, near his hands, fish shoot.
When spring melt comes, he'll thaw into his enchanted life,
the surface that's sustained him will finally break up,
he'll dip and sweep his hand, sweep the puny kingdom
of his face into the running stream, as if he could free
himself from himself, come alive in flooding loss,
stooped, astonished that love feels so posthumous now.

Dancing in the Dark

Pain and ecstasy kissing, tongues and spit and all. What's happening to the room? All that broken glass in your back and legs, but keep at it, get lost in the motion and the pain will release you and become aboriginal glass, shape-shifting melting sand. Probation again, Mister Lucky. Get so far into your body you feel outside it. Swing, salsa, samba: Dionysus, necromancer, amped, waving his dick, always on the move, and his torchlight gang follows wherever he leads, and he's out of control. Get close enough to him to get hurt. (Cue "Neutron Dance.") Smell yourself all over your partner, tear up your knee, go out in style. Stay in motion or you're finished. *"Keep movin' on / I'm goin' on."* Like poetry: to stay in motion. Who wants poetry like freeze-dried coffee? Poets, keep it close, loose, sweaty. In the 1920s, Bantu, Yoruba, and Ewe slaves formed religious brotherhoods, *irmandades,* that beat drums, sang, and danced themselves into trance states, rubbing against each other. The African word for "rubbing navels"—*semba!*

Their Old Knives

For the livers and lasagna, the tomatoes planted
in broken concrete backyard plots in spring,
when Havana's tropicals and flamingo heat
migrated toward our own city summer,
for Jersey beans loving 9th Street's market sun
where women frowned and men sold glory,
and August's soggy long summer skies boomed
and purpled before rain fell on our heads
like an end of time, for artichoke points and plums,
for watermelon hissing back at this blade
that once turned its other cheek to day-old
brick-oven bread, your fine uneven edges
faintly silvered once I diamond-steel
their ground, used-up years of rust and gray…
Be ready for my needs, to do the work you know,
to answer hunger at odd times like these,
around midnight, or six hours later, the cantaloupe
or breakfast crust, then lunchtime's cold cuts,
dinner's cutlets, scunions, beets, you knives,
and the silver dollars and unlikely crystal flutes…
the precious few things, except for their lives,
that I saved from the house of the dead,
where they argued, flashed you like batons
at their enemy, themselves, before or after food,
be ready for whatever waits in half-dark now,
for telltale chance, or fatal cherishing.

That Night at Baldini's

As if no sky hung outside, no nature there,
      only here inside the viewing room: putrid fresh
mums and lilies, wreath-bunting in loving memory, ceiling
      a puttied celestial blue no sky ever was.
It felt as if it had already happened, the entry and descent.
      The older brother's bleached face, maquette finger bones
dressed with pearled rosaries, the hushed receiving line
      conjoining his big silence, speech's juices drained,
laid out in the box's jewelry-tray bedding, in that other life,
      called life, that our waiting breaths believe waits for us, too.
From among the wishers, the whisperers and consorts who inhaled with me
      those wet humus smells aroused under Baldini's parlor sky
wherein nature nothinged lay, the younger brother advances
      and fleshes out the scene, reaching toward the plump raised lid:
to go down there with him, not let him go alone—who of us knows
      how alone, how that will be, what tincture, taste, sniff lives on
beyond the senses, what delusion we imagine so fine?—
      so first elbow, shoulder, knee, foot, talking to himself,
(unweeping, fortified by love) he climbs into the box, to go down,
      brother on brother, down to all the others, whoever they are,
the bumbles of the dead as if inside walls or a stage-trap underfoot,
      down through the trick-bottomed Houdini device
to foundation joists and soil, tree roots, silicates and spores
      and spongy membranes, dirt's intestines, to all the others
gone before, amassed in channels like nebular gangs
      of dark matter that holds our bodies together right now,
their bellings and keens, calling for us or telling us to stay away.

He went that way until others pulled him back:
You have to let him go! No, you don't, not until you go find out
for yourself, ask away the years, the longings. And now
you're finally with that sad brother who spoke so little, who lived
in shade until he became shade of his flesh shamed
by alien human likeness in the box, the lacquered big-mouth box,
down stainless corridors to pooled chambered dark below,
like a nothing air one falls into, weightless, stillborn, slowed, unbound,
where neither of you now has anything to say to us.

Renovations

going on everywhere
in summer's cold wind
winging through hollies.
Banana plants flap
like canvas sails
above a dugout cellar
where Latino boys shoulder
cans of dirt, rocks.
Three doors down
more or less...
things feel approximate
like my window draft haunted
by the "Aura amorosa" aria
I've listened and whistled to
too much this morning
that renews me bitterly
sweet like the mug
on the pit bull
neighborhood kids adore,
recovering from surgery
while his owner Mike or Fred
three doors down
lays Italian tiles
on his rebuilt stoop.
There's a small tremble
in the familiar orders
that keep us, that we keep,
the ocean's big breath

through high treetops,

then lower down

a housepainter's billowing

black nets suck and mash

above those Michoacanos

digging a duplex foundation

for New World gold:

all those respirations

in the pushy nonstop wind

thrown like a threshold

between us and the trench,

us and whatever's there

underworld or overworld

where certain friends say

they will, at the end

of the things of this world,

be laid to rest,

but (I say) what rest?

About the Author

W.S. Di Piero is the author of numerous volumes of poetry, essays on culture and personal experience, and translations. His previous book of poems is *Chinese Apples: New and Selected Poems*. Other recent publications include *When Can I See You Again? New Art Writings* and *Night of Shooting Stars: The Selected Poems of Leonardo Sinisgalli*. He's a frequent contributor to *The Threepenny Review* and writes a regular column on art for an independent weekly newspaper, the *San Diego Reader*. He lives in San Francisco.

Since 1972, Copper Canyon Press has fostered the work of emerging, established, and world-renowned poets for an expanding audience. The Press thrives with the generous patronage of readers, writers, booksellers, librarians, teachers, students, and funders — everyone who shares the belief that poetry is vital to language and living.

MAJOR SUPPORT HAS BEEN PROVIDED BY:

The Paul G. Allen Family Foundation

Amazon.com

Anonymous

Diana and Jay Broze

Beroz Ferrell & The Point, LLC

Golden Lasso, LLC

Gull Industries, Inc.
on behalf of William and Ruth True

Lannan Foundation

Rhoady and Jeanne Marie Lee

National Endowment for the Arts

Cynthia Lovelace Sears and Frank Buxton

Washington State Arts Commission

Charles and Barbara Wright

To learn more about underwriting
Copper Canyon Press titles, please call
360-385-4925 ext. 103

The Chinese character for poetry is made up of two parts: "word" and "temple." It also serves as pressmark for Copper Canyon Press.

The poems are set in Fournier, designed by Monotype Type Foundry in 1924, based on types cut by Pierre Simon Fournier circa 1742.
Book design and composition by Phil Kovacevich.
Printed on archival-quality paper at McNaughton & Gunn, Inc.